P9-CFW-369

Please visit our web site at: www.garethstevens.com
For a free color catalog describing Gareth Stevens Publishing's
list of high-quality books and multimedia programs, call
1-800-542-2595 (USA) or 1-800-387-3178 (Canada).
Gareth Stevens Publishing's fax: (414) 332-3567.

Library of Congress Cataloging-in-Publication Data available upon request from publisher.
Fax (414) 336-0157 for the attention of the Publishing Records Department.

ISBN 0-8368-4109-3

This North American edition first published in 2004 by
Gareth Stevens Publishing
A World Almanac Education Group Company
330 West Olive Street, Suite 100
Milwaukee, WI 53212 USA

Original copyright © 1995 by Creative Teaching Press, Inc.
First published in the United States in 1995 as *The Crayola® Counting Book*
in the *Learn to Read -- Read to Learn Math Series* by Creative Teaching
Press, Inc., P.O. Box 2723, Huntington Beach, CA 92647-0723.

Gareth Stevens series editor: Dorothy L. Gibbs
Gareth Stevens series designer: Kami M. Koenig

Printed in the United States of America

1 2 3 4 5 6 7 8 9 08 07 06 05 04

Crayola® is a registered trademark of Binney & Smith, makers of Crayola® products. The publishers
would like to extend special thanks to Binney & Smith for their cooperation in the production of this book.

Crayola® COUNTING

Written by Rozanne Lanczak Williams
Photographed by Michael Jarrett

I CAN
+ DO
MATH

Gareth Stevens Publishing
A WORLD ALMANAC EDUCATION GROUP COMPANY

Open the box. The crayons fall out.

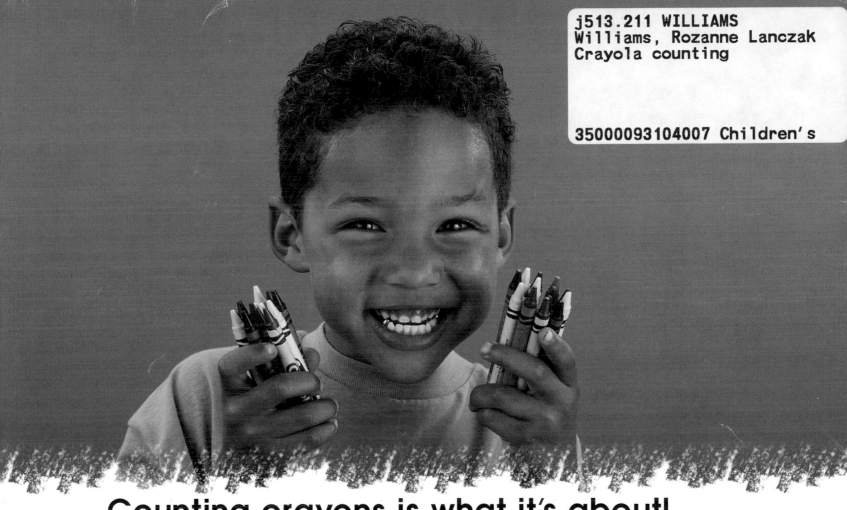

Counting crayons is what it's about!

5

Count the red crayons. Count the blues.

Count by fives. Count by twos.

Count the crayons in the smallest pack.

Now, count the crayons in the biggest stack.

Count the orange crayons. Count the brown.

Count the crayons that are on the ground.

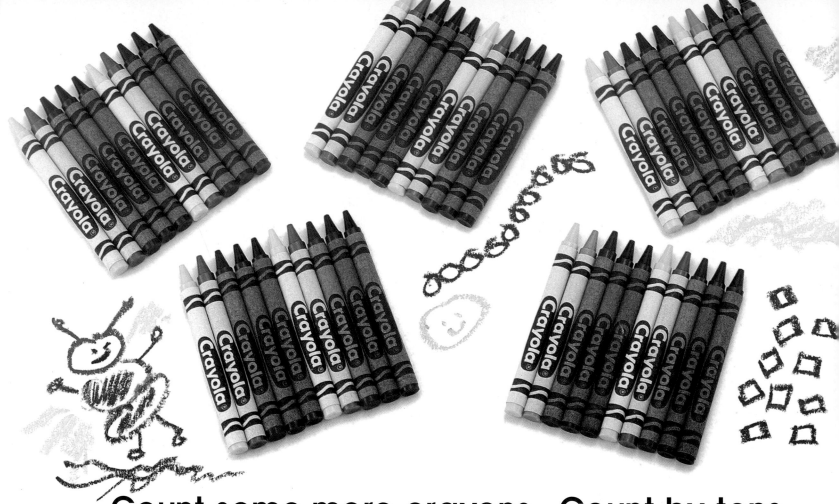

Count some more crayons. Count by tens.

Did you count one hundred? Count again!

Crayons can be counted

by twos, fives, or tens.

But the

BEST

thing about crayons . . .

16

is drawing with them!

18

It's fun to draw pictures and color them, too.

Now let's see . . .